I0011284

Search Engine Optimization Secrets For Small Businesses

A Quick-Start Reference Guide

by Matt Goodwin

www.SEOSECRETSBOOK.com

Disclaimer

Please use this book and the ideas expressed in the book at your own risk.

I am sharing my experiences. I am not associated with any search engine or directory.

Ethical SEO does not promote any practices that trick, fool or deceive a search engine and is based on quality content and natural linking (links that are given to a website freely and without compensation of any kind).

Unethical SEO (Aka Black Hat SEO or Gorilla SEO) are also discussed in this book. I offer both for your benefit in order to show you what can be done and when SEO techniques cross the line to SPAM. I recommend staying away from unethical SEO as your website can be banned from search engines for using such techniques. A well designed website with quality, unique content is always the best practice.

Something to remember when reading this book...
Information in this book is based on my 15+ years of SEO experience and my own judgment. My opinions will obviously differ from those of other SEO experts. Some information in this book may not match the opinions of *any* other SEO expert.

This book is a reflects my beliefs based upon past experiences. This book is meant to be used as a guide. use caution when implementing any of the ideas in this book.

All company names used in this book are registered trademarks of their respective owners which I am not affiliated with in any way.

Table of Contents

Acknowledgement

I would like to thank my mother, Connie Robillard, for urging me to finish this book. After six months of frustrating writing I tabled my project. My mother is an author, psychotherapist and also my client. It is I who built her first website and turned her into a believer of the power of search engine optimization.

It is because of her positive attitude and support that gave me the encouragement I needed to take this project off the shelf and finish it.

Dedication

This book is dedicated to all small business owners. I have been inspired by individuals who risk it all to make it big in America.

Introduction

My name is Matt Goodwin, I have been optimizing websites since 1996. At the time, I worked for a small business that replaced automotive engines in Nashua NH. It was a competitive business, in fact it was so competitive that a study was done that found the cost to get each customer was around $175.00 in advertising and marketing, so we were always looking for less expensive advertising solutions. We put a lot of effort into newspaper ads, yellow pages, television, radio, magazines, classified ads, you name it.

The shop owner and I discussed the need for online advertizing to compete with our competitors. Hiring a website designer would have been expensive. The owner's wife worked for a high tech company. She took the time to teach me the basics of html. From there I built the company's first website. It was at a time when most businesses didn't use the internet as an advertizing tool. The website I built brought in more customers at a lower cost. It was a success!

The process of building the website encouraged me to learn more about it. The competitive side of me quickly took over and I wanted to get our website above the competition's website on search engines. After a lot of hard work I accomplished this goal and could see the future for me in what is now called search engine optimization (SEO).

With the Internet coming to life it created an opportunity for small businesses to have the same image as a large corporation's on the Internet. I wanted to help small business owners crawl out of the slump and get out there and compete with these big businesses with little or no money.

In September 2001 I lost my job at the engine shop, the business was booming. The owner was getting older and had enough. He decided to close the doors despite the booming business. I wasn't quite ready to start my Internet business so I found another job as an automotive service manager. Just 3 months later in December 2001 I was laid off from the new job and was forced to start a cleaning business, handyman service and a pet sitting business. I did all of these things just to survive. I found myself once again turning to the Internet to promote these services.

While I worked hard the money still wasn't enough and I began selling on eBay in my downtime. I enjoyed the Internet side of what I was doing much more than the labor intensive cleaning business. Everything together seemed to be enough to pay the bills but my efforts felt too divided. I felt like I wasn't able to do any one of the jobs effectively because I was doing a little of everything. I wanted to focus my efforts on my Internet business.

In November 2002 I was diagnosed with Hurthle-Cell Thyroid Cancer. It was a huge blow for me. I thought I was indestructible up until that point. All the wind I had in my sails was gone. I had no job, working 5 different angles to survive, no money, no Internet business as I had dreamed of and now cancer. Fight or flight was in full effect... Fight it was, game on! I was forced to start my Internet business right then as I was unable to work. Dr. visits, surgery, radiation treatment, follow ups, daily blood tests, scans... it all came at me at once. I took my last bit of money and risked it all (all $440 of it) on starting the web design/SEO business I dreamed of. I did everything I could to get the business off the ground while I fought the cancer war. I was beaten down to a shell of a man. I was weak, pale, sick... but I fought and just kept fighting. When the dust cleared I got lucky. The sun was shining and I won both of these battles in my life. I thought "my god, if I can do this while fighting cancer anyone can do it!" You just have to want it bad enough.

Today, I still own my web design/SEO business and clients find me through referrals. I don't bother optimizing my own website anymore because I get a ton of referral business from past clients. I have clients in very competitive markets like maid services in New York City and vacation rentals in Hawaii just to name a few.

Things are much different these days in the SEO world than they were 15 years ago. Getting good search engine rankings is much more difficult. Search engine optimization is a lot of work. It takes a lot of time and a lot of effort but most importantly, it takes persistence. You have to crave it. You have to crave it like I did. So do whatever you need to do to get motivated. Myself, I drive to the seacoast here in New Hampshire and I look at the multi-million dollar mansions that dot the seacoast. That's what I want! It motivates me to come back to my desk and kick butt! It's important that you capture what motivates you and use it to your advantage.

There is no magic bullet to SEO, its hard work. Getting visitors to your website takes a million little things that you do for your website collectively.

Roll up your sleeves and get reading, you have work to do if you're going to turn your online business into a success...

A Note About Search Engines

Search engines are as close to human thinking as you can imagine. They use closely guarded algorithms that determine how results are served up. They know when a visitor likes the site they're reading, they know how they found it, what search terms they used to find it, if they bookmarked it, how long they stayed on the site, which links they clicked on, where they went after entering the site, if they left the site, if they left the site they know which page they left on, if they did a search again to find better information, where the visitor is from, what type of Internet they are using, which browser they're using, and the list goes on...   Search engines are amazing! Well, most of them anyway. Be sure you always create your content for humans, but then add a few extra keywords and keyword phrases to let the search engines know what the content is about.

Most importantly, make sure that the information you provide is interesting, doesn't give away too much info too fast, but lures the reader to keep reading to get what they want and is entertaining in some way and encourages them to click another link to keep reading, view photos, or to get information about a similar topic.

The Basics
(A Must Read)

In the mid 1990's only a few small business had websites. Those that did gave their potential customers instant trust in their company. Having worked for a company that had a website, one that I created for them, I remember hearing the customer's tone of voice and confidence change instantly as soon as I told them we had a website. At the time it was magical and did wonders for a small business. Customers were educated consumers by the time they dialed our phone number.

Today, with the almost endless amounts of tools out there that make it easy to create your own website, many small businesses have a website. It seems like everyone you meet these days has a website. While this makes the Internet a wealth of information, it has a downfall. The downside to all these websites and information on the Internet is that it makes it harder to get traffic to your own website. This is why SEO is so important, just having a website is not enough. I explain this to my clients who want me to build a website for them. My first question to them is "Where do you intend on getting traffic from?" This is the problem with the build-your-own website services. Many of them so not explain the need for proper SEO methods to get traffic to your website. So small businesses invest loads of time in building the site and then they wait for the traffic to arrive... most times it never comes unless they were lucky enough to have a website that became viral.

No matter which program or service you used to design and maintain your website, you should be able to apply the instructions I have outlined. While I cannot give you instructions for every web design software or site building service, I would recommend taking it one step at a time and learn how to make the changes. This is where the wealth of information on the Internet can help you more than I can (i.e.: If I mention changing the title of your web page, just do a search for "how to change the title of my web page using (enter the name of your software or site building service). This should get you the information you need. If not, there is always the dreaded tech support, but at least you will know what you are looking to do when you call them.

A few things to remember about SEO...

First (and I'm sure it's no surprise) the internet is an ever-changing world and so is SEO. You will have days where you realize that some of the SEO work you have been doing is not as beneficial as it once was or is not recognized by search engines any longer. When a search engine changes its algorithms they do not email the world to tell them what they have done and why. Most of their technology is closely guarded, so it takes time for the changes to trickle out as SEO's test a few sites or a few web pages and see how the search engine responds. Because of these changes I would recommend not getting too heavy into one method of SEO and be ready to make changes and adjust your techniques on the fly.

I have known many SEO experts over the years and they push their latest craze or breakthrough on me and want me to join in and invest thousands of dollars and a lot of time to their new found methods. But I see things a little differently... If these people discover a new SEO "trick" to get rich, you can bet your booty the search engines are already all over it. Search engines didn't get to where they are now by being slow on new discoveries. Chances are they not only knew about it before the SEO experts did but have already addressed the problem.

If you want to play it safe and give the search engines what they want then give them interesting, quality, unique content.... everything else is a risk!

Secondly, I also feel it's necessary to say what our parents have said for years "do one thing and do it well!" That rings true in my head everyday and I wish I had listened. I have made every mistake imaginable, but this is great for you. Who better to learn from than someone who has made such monumental mistakes. Hopefully I can steer you away from some of these very costly mistakes I made.

Additionally, it's best to focus your efforts on one website for best results. Those who try to focus on managing too many different websites will have a challenge getting any of them to the top. At one point I had nearly 60 websites and all of them suffered. I just didn't have the time, especially since the big changes came with the major search engines. You really need to stay focused on the project at hand, even when things start to pick up. Never assume your website will take care of itself when the traffic starts coming in and head towards another project. This is when things will deteriorate. Having a couple projects is one thing, but to be successful you should work on your website no less than once a week, every day is better, every hour is best. The more frequently you make changes and add content the more frequently search engines will come visit your site and index new information. So stay focused and expect a long haul to the finish line. It takes time to be successful online Be prepared to commit time to your website at least weekly.

Also be sure to remember your site must be interesting to the reader. Search engines know when they send you a visitor and your site disappointed them with wrong information, too cluttered, too many ads or not enough information. Make your site clean and easy to read and navigate with limited advertising, avoiding pop-up/pop-under ads if possible. Be informative and captivating always give plenty of details. Visit other websites that rank high for the keywords you are targeting. Think about the types of things that you like and don't like on those websites. Focus on getting users more and better information than what you see on those sites. The information on your site MUST be better, more accurate, more descriptive, easier to understand and of higher quality if you want your web page/site to be competitive to these other websites.

Be sure not to aim too high with your projects. By this I mean be realistic in selecting the keywords you want to target. You may find that starting off with a lesser searched keyword phrase is easier to make money with than going for the gold right off the bat. The higher you aim, the more work and cost involved and the longer it will take to reach this goal. The typical person or business does not have the finances or the time to invest in such a project. So rather than trying to rank high for the keyword "cleaning service" maybe you focus on "office cleaning service Raleigh NC." This better targets your business and will be easier to get some traffic from search engines. If you are successful getting decent rankings for "cleaning services" you will spend a lot of time working on this and will end up with traffic you don't actually want. You will get emails from all over the world to provide cleaning services. I will get more into keywords later.

Getting Started

Before you begin your SEO work, be sure you have read the previous sections of this book. It is important to understand everything before you begin making changes to your website. I can't tell you how many times I got excited about a new SEO technique and jumped right into a project only to find out I got ahead of myself and ended up having to re-do the entire project.

Keyword Research

The first step with any SEO project to ALWAYS research your keywords and market before doing any optimization work! Spend a lot of time with this and don't rush into the SEO. If you do I can almost guarantee it will come back to bite you and you will be making changes and doing work over wishing you took my advice here.

There are some great keyword selector tools out there. Just do a search for "keyword selector tool."

I also use search suggestions when fine-tuning my keywords. I would recommend reading the "Search Suggestions" section of this book before finishing your keyword research.

Using Search Suggestions to Your Advantage

Many search engines now offer search suggestions. Search suggestions are the search phrases that appear when you begin to type your search query in the search box. The more you type, the suggestions change to help you refine your search. These search suggestions can be very useful for some people, others really don't like it and turn off the feature in their toolbar.

Doing a search for the search term "Leaf Rake Metal" may bring up the following suggestions:

When the word "Leaf" is typed in the following suggestions may appear:
leaf identification
leaf blower
leaf blower ban
leaf antenna

When you add the word "Rake" to your search term, "Leaf Rake" the search suggestions will get closer to what you're looking for and will bring up search suggestions like:
leaf rake for pool
leaf rake for tractor
leaf rake for swimming pool

When you add the final word in this example "metal" the search suggestions become even more refined:
metal leaf rake
plastic metal leaf rake
large metal leaf rake
metal tine leaf rake

Like it or not people are using search suggestions when they search. With that said you should use this tool to your advantage to get some ideas on what you can create your website content about.

Go to a few major search engines and start searching the main keyword for your site. Start with the main keyword for your site and look at the suggestions that come up for that word. Then after that word hit the space bar and then type in only one letter, start with A and the suggestions will change showing the next words that begin with A." Then erase the letter A and then type in B and see what comes up. Go right through the entire alphabet. You will see a few things that catch your eye and it will give you some new ideas. What I do is take those search terms that come up in the search suggestion and make a new web page for each one of them and focus my keywords on each phrase for a single web page. Make sure you create a page for each keyword phrase and write plenty of quality, unique content for each page you create. Never just throw stuff up on your website just to get the search phrase on your website. If you do, make sure you go back afterwards and fix it but its best to not do it at all.

So what is the advantage of this?

The advantage is simple, if search engines are suggesting these searches for users, people are more likely to use it. It might be because it gave them an idea they didn't consider searching for. Whatever the reason, you want to have your website tuned into it and ready to give them that exact information. When you give the user the exact info they want they will read more about it on your site, then you can direct them to your product or service on another part of your website.

How Domain Names Can Affect SEO

Search engine optimization starts right at the business name and domain name of your website. Don't worry too much if your business name or website domain name is already registered, but if you haven't yet registered your domain name always consider a domain name with keywords. Search engines are able to recognize words within the domain name. For example, if you sell metal leaf rakes, consider a domain like MetalLeafRakes.com. Registering a domain that is accurate to the products or services you sell will help your site greatly. Make sure you build the site and add content to that keyword rich domain name. You can then register your business name as a domain name and forward it to your keyword rich domain name. This way your business cards and other print ads can use that domain name but search engines will be indexing your keyword rich domain name website.

When selecting a domain name keep in mind that search engines rank brand sites higher. So if your business name is Orlando Tree Service, your business will rank higher for the search term " Orlando Tree Service." A good reason to include good keywords in the name of your business!

In the early 2000's people had to use hyphens in their domain names so search engines could "read" the words in the domain name. I still have a few of these domains myself. Today, there is no need to hyphenate a domain name but it can still be done in cases where the non-hyphenated domain has already been registered. Just keep in mind that it's not much fun when you have to tell someone what the web address is. If you're having trouble finding an available domain name with keywords in it, try using other words with it, like: MetalLeafRakeMan.com, MetalLeafRakeCity.com, or better yet, add another keyword to it like DurableMetalLeafRakes.com, BestMetalLeafRakes.com, MetalLeafRakeReviews.com, etc. Spend some time and make sure you register the right domain name.

When someone does a search for "Metal Leaf Rakes" chances are, your site will be at or near the top with the correct optimization work. Sometimes these keyword rich domain name sites may start near the top when you first register it and put your site up, then slide down to page 3 or 4 without any further optimization unless the site is doing well and people are using the site. So don't stop at the domain name!

If you are worried about your business name not being your domain name, you can have the best of both worlds by registering both a keyword rich domain name and your business name as a domain name. Forwarding the business name domain name to the keyword rich domain name. This will need to be done wherever your register the domain name. Make sure all SEO work happens on the keyword rich domain name though. This way the keyword rich domain will come up on searches and people typing in your business domain name will be seamlessly forwarded to the optimized website and if done correctly, no one will even notice.

Note: Never place the same website at two different domain names. Duplicated sites will not do well, and if caught can be removed from a search engine's results.

An interesting story: In the 90's my brother wanted to start a piano moving business. He knows a lot about business and knew the business name was important. I talked to him about the importance of the domain name too before he registered the business name. He considered it all and then came up with the business name "Piano Movers" but the lady at the State of NH Corporate Division (where you register a business name in New Hampshire) said no because it was too general, so then he came up with "www.PianoMoversInc.com" as a business name! The lady at the state corporate office was a little taken back and had to check with a supervisor. It was approved and they called him a genius. I have to agree, his business name was perfect as is the domain name. Using this as an example you can see how his business name reflects keywords that will be used on his website. As a result, his site ranked higher for "piano movers" (currently #2 in Google). In addition, people know his website address and it saves text in signage and other advertising. He never has to explain what he does, it is perfect for SEO... the name was perfect! The business succeeded and is still in business today running all over New England, New York and New Jersey with daily trips to Boston. Not all the credit goes to his business name and domain name, he knows his business well and that's why he remains in business even through a bad economy.

Another thing to mention about domain names is that there has been some speculation about the amount of time your domain in registered for impacting your search engine rankings. It is assumed that the longer your domain is registered the search engines see this as a form of credibility and stability. I personally have never had any luck with this technique. I have tested it with 5 different websites and none of the websites were effected either way during my 4 year period of testing.

How Website Hosting Can Affect SEO

If you have a few different websites you work with you may want to consider separating them onto different servers. Combine this with using different names and contact information in your domain name registration information. This way you can link them together for added link popularity. See the Link Popularity section for more information on the benefits of links. Search engines know when you have a collection of websites. If you keep them completely separate you will have a better chance of those links adding some link popularity to your sites, just don't overdo the links!

Don't make a website filled with affiliate ads. I said it a million times and I will say it again... Quality, unique content will win every time!

Page loading time can also affect your website's ranking on search engines. If your pages load slowly due to huge file sizes, search engines know that people will get frustrated and will likely rank your site lower. Search engines will also take note of people leaving your site or hitting the back button as people don't want to wait for your slow pages to load. This could also be interpreted at poor quality content and again negatively affect your site. I have seen many amateur-created websites that look fairly nice and are well-written but no one took the time to bump the image file size down and are displaying images on their site that are as large as 1-2 MB. Be sure the information provided with your text content (like photos) are optimized for faster loading times.

Server speed is also an important part of optimization. Be sure you select a quality hosting service provider. Search engines will rank your site lower if your page loading time is slow, even if this is a server issue. No one wants to hang around and wait for a page to load, spend the extra few bucks and get a decent hosting service provider! My company offers fast hosting if you need a better web hosting option (ModernConcepts.ORG).

Optimizing Your Website

Optimizing your website is the most important part of creating your online presence. The following sections are broken down into segments to make it easy to understand.

Website Content

Web page content is the most important part of your SEO efforts. Quality, unique content is crucial. First of all no matter how tempting, never, ever, ever, ever copy content from another website! It's not only illegal but it is a waste of time. Search engines know if the content is duplicated and will not consider the duplicated content as important and it will sink on the search results. Search engines don't want to serve up the same content on search results because no one wants to see the same thing over and over again. Would you be happy if I copied the information in this book from a another book you just read? Of course not. The same goes for search engine results.

Search engines also know when your content is superior to similar websites. SEO is much more than just throwing keywords in your content, throwing up some ads and moving on. Spend the time to get this right and the content will continue to work for you, try to skim through this time consuming process just to get it done and you will be scratching your head later on wondering why no visitors come to your website. It's that simple, I can't stress it enough!

The best content is created by gathering information away from your computer. Take photos, videos and write in-depth articles about specific topics. For example, on my tourism website I go out and gather information about different attractions. I don't go to another website to gather the information. As a matter of fact I try to *stay away* from websites that have the same information that I am attempting to gather. Mainly because I don't want that content stuck in my head and I don't want someone else's opinions to influence my own.

In one of the sections of my tourism website, I offer information about waterfalls in the state of New Hampshire. I get a list of waterfalls together that I want to tackle, grab my camera, my GPS, and my video camera, I get in my truck and drive a couple hours to the trail and hike it myself and make notes about problems and cool things I encounter. I take photos and videos and GPS locations so that others can find the waterfall. Now I could have just gone to Google Maps and grabbed a GPS location, took a photo from someone else and learn about it and re-wrote the text but that is not the way to go at all (nor is it legal).

To apply this to different businesses, let's say you're selling leaf rakes. Most people don't think much about the quality of a leaf rake, but some do and we will use it as an example here.

So, if you take all the leaf rakes you sell and use them all to test them, check the handles, does the company use quality wood for handles or do they use junky wood or plastic? Are the plastic rakes heavy duty and flexible or do they break easily? Do the metal rakes bend? Don't be afraid to video tape your products (or services) in action. Find the ones you liked and write down why you liked them, basically reviewing your own products or service. People like product reviews and they like to see the product or service in action and detailed photos of every inch of the product. If you are able to add a section on your site for people to add their own reviews that will also help.

If you offer services it might be best to offer free advice or information about the products you use.

The bottom line to creating quality, unique content is to offer the details that people just can't get anywhere else.

Your page content should match the title, description and keyword tags as well as the heading tags within your html meta tags. Refer to the section called "Heading Tags" for more information on this. Always double check to make sure everything matches.

Content should also be changed often. Add to the content as new information becomes available.
Be very specific! Garden rakes on one page, leaf rakes on another, plastic leaf rakes on another, metal leaf rakes, etc... Keeping each page to a very specific product or service is important. Make sure you type unique text for each item. It is best to have over 500 words about each product or service (on each web page).

Search engines read like humans do... from left to right. So the most important words should be first. The trick is getting it to read correctly while do this. You will need to fiddle around with your text a bit to make it all work, but the time spent will be worth it in the end.

Text given extra attention like the use of heading tags, bullets and bold text will be given more weight by search engines.

Forums

Forums can be a great way of getting better search engine rankings and rankings for topics you didn't consider adding to your website. Basically, to the SEO a forum is a great tool and the people who post on your forum are your free employees. People post topics on your forum and then search engines pick it up and index it. This keeps information on your website fresh, constantly being updated by your "free employees." The more people post, the more frequently search engines will come and spider your website and index the new content.

Having a quality forum is key to your success if you plan on adding a forum to your website, so spare no expense here. Stay away from free forum software. I have tried free forums and had very little success using it to get more people to the website. I switched one of my websites to a better quality forum and saw the difference almost immediately and kicked myself for not doing it sooner. Recently I have been using VBulletin for all of my forums which has worked very well with my SEO efforts.

Before you add a forum to your website, make sure that your site should have one. If you sell leaf rakes or something else just as boring, you might want to sit this one out. Unless you can come up with some genius idea to make rakes and raking fun and make people want to talk about it.

For other more interesting products and services, a forum should help you in some way. Even if you offer landscaping services and everyone posting on your forum isn't from your area, they are still generating fresh, unique content for you, so your website should still reap the benefits. If someone asks "why is my grass brown," then you or another user of the forum answers the question, this is the type of quality content that search engines look for. Maybe they titled their post "Why is my grass brown?" From there, a search engine picks up this new post and includes it in their index.

When a search engine user asks that same question, that forum post should come up somewhere in the search results. The position of your site coming up for that phrase will depend on many other factors, but it will be there somewhere.

Another good idea when it comes to forums is to give the users free advice. Your site will have new, changing content and search engine love that! For informative posts and replies, other websites will also link to your forum pages increasing your link popularity.

The use of a forum can be a very strategic move if done correctly.

Using Bullets

Bullets can be used to place emphasis on certain keywords or phrases. Search engines may see these words as more important since you have singled them out on your website as important enough words and phrases that you felt it necessary to put them in a bulleted list. When using bullets, it is best to not use images as bullets. The correct way to use bullets for SEO purposes is to create the bullets with html code instead of images.

```
<ul>
        <li>Important Keyword Phrase Here</li>
        <li>Another Important Keyword Phrase Here</li>
        <li> Another Important Keyword Phrase Here </li>
        <li> Another Important Keyword Phrase Here </li>
</ul>
```

Another way is to use this code:

• Keyword Phrase Here

Some will argue that the latter of the two examples is best for SEO, I say either one works just as good.

Using Bold Text

The use of bold text is another way to put emphasis on your important keywords and phrases. Don't go too crazy using bold text though or search engines will ignore your use of bold text altogether. Bold text is great for the text on paragraph headings, headers and even text within a paragraph that you would like to be seen as important text. Search engines will also consider that text as potentially important but again, don't overuse it!

META Tags

META tags are no longer widely recognized by search engines. I still use them because there are still some search engines out there that recognize them. I also believe the title tag is still important. Some search engines are now disregarding the title tag and using the page content to generate a title. So I will give you some pointers on how these tags work.

Depending on which program you use to create or edit your website, you may need to edit raw html code. If you use a web based program, most companies will give you tools to edit these fields without the need to edit the html code directly.

Page Title Tag

The title is what usually appears in the SERPs (search engine results pages). The page title also appears in your browser's top section once on the page. The page title tag of each of your web pages can be very important. Sometimes search engines replace your title tag with one they feel better represents the information contained on the web page. (Remember, search engines cater to the person searching, not the website owner). I always use accurate keyword rich title tags for my pages. Even though accurate, I still find search engines replacing some of my titles.

Most times, making an adjustment here can move your site (up or down) on the search engines. So be careful with this tag but also make sure you make the best use of it! Also be sure you never use the same title for multiple web pages. Make sure every page on your website has completely unique text throughout, including page title.

If your title tag says "Home Page" or is not entered at all, you can make a big difference in your website's ranking fairly quickly by adding a keyword rich title to your web page. Be careful not to add more than 70 characters to your title tag. Adding more than 70 characters won't do much good and excessive or spammy title tags could be ignored altogether by many search engines.

When creating a title tag be sure to do some research on good keywords for your product or service. Keep in mind that search engines read left to right as humans do, so words that appear on the left or first in a sentence are given more weight. In almost all cases, it is best to not use your business name first in a title tag. For example, let's say your company name is John's Yard Products and your website sells yard products like rakes (garden rakes and leaf rakes). You don't want your title on your rakes page to look like this:

"John's Yard Products: Best Prices on Yard Products"

Your rakes page will rank higher for "John's Yard Products" but you won't be selling rakes to any customers that don't know exactly **who** they are looking for. People who want to buy rakes will search for "rakes," "leaf rakes" or "garden rakes."

A better title for your rakes page would look like this:
"Leaf Rakes and Garden Rakes by John's Yard Products"

To take this a step further, use a keyword tool and put the higher searched rakes first in the title tag.

Local vs. global thinking: When I think local, Here in New Hampshire dethatching rakes and leaf rakes are more searched than other rakes but globally the numbers vary. If you're selling globally you will want to take this under consideration. Also, the word "dethatching" is a longer word. You might be better off with 2 or 3 smaller words, than 1 or 2 big ones. Of course the word "rakes" is a much more commonly searched word than any other phrase containing rakes. So how do you handle this? One way is like this:

"Rakes: Leaf Rakes, Garden Rakes and Dethatching Rakes"

Notice I left out the business name entirely. If people are looking for your business they will search harder trying to find you if needed. Your business name will be within the content of your site anyway so most likely you won't be too hard to find. Be sure to add your business to online maps, like Google Maps. This will help your business come up when someone is looking for you.

Also note that I only used 53 characters instead of the 70 allowed characters. I did this because I don't want to spam the search engines with keywords. Try not to use more than one comma in the title (if any) and don't use a keyword more than 3 times. I maxed out on both on the example above. If you feel you really need your business name in the title (brick and mortar businesses this might be desired but don't feel you have to do it), be sure to add it to the end of the title not the beginning, like this:

"Leaf Rakes, Garden Rakes and Dethatching Rakes by John's Yard Products"

The example above has exactly 70 characters. Why did I take out the first word "rakes?" The keyword alone is very competitive. People usually search for that one word, then see too much junk that they didn't want and find they need to narrow their search to find exactly what they wanted. So just because the word "rakes" is a lot more of a searched word, don't be fooled too much by the stats. You are better off with highly targeted traffic. And if you're business name is more important, that's a sacrifice you will need to make. You may want to test it with and without your business name to see how the search engines react and if the same amount of people are still finding you using your business name.

Many search engines have added search suggestions while you type in the search box of a major search engine. So now things like song lyrics come up and other unrelated suggestions when you're searching for "rakes." So as people type the word "rakes" in the search box, they are looking at the suggestions popping up and when they see what they want, they click on it. If they don't see what they want and instead see things like song lyrics, they are refining their search as they type until they see more related suggestions.

For more info about search suggestion tool, see the section in the book called "Search Suggestions."

Creating a title tag:
To create a title tag, most web design tools will put it in the "page properties" section of the software, like Microsoft FrontPage and Expression Web. If you can't find the area to edit this information you may have to do it manually by adding it to the raw HTML code and placing it within the head tags near the top of the HTML code for each web page:

Here is an example of the title tag code:

```
<head>
<title>Your Page Title Goes Here</title>
</head>
```

Description Tag

The description tag is still recognized by some search engines but for the most part has been eliminated. Again, I still use it for the few search engines that still use this information. The description tag should be no more than 160 characters. Using the example of "metal leaf rakes," try to start the sentence with a keyword phrase like "Metal leaf rakes are the most durable...." " Using your most important keyword phrase in the beginning of the sentence.

To create a description tag, most web design tools will put it in the "page properties" section of the software, like Microsoft FrontPage and Expression Web. If you can't find the area to edit this information you may have to do it manually by adding it to the raw HTML code and placing it within the head tags near the top of the html code for the web page:

Here is an example of the description tag code:

```
<head>
<meta name="description" CONTENT="Your web page description goes here.">
</head>
```

Keywords Tag

The keywords tag is the least recognized tag by search engines currently but I do recommend still using it, just don't bother to abuse it as it's not worth it.

Add no more than 155 characters (about 10 keywords or phrases separated by commas). Don't use the same keyword more than 3 times in the same keyword tag. Abusing this tag will do you absolutely no good at all and may actually harm your rankings.

To create a keyword tag, most web design tools will put it in the "page properties" section of the software, like Microsoft FrontPage and Expression Web. If you can't find the area to edit this information you may have to do it manually by adding it to the raw HTML code and placing it within the head tags near the top of the page:

Here is an example of the keywords tag code:

```
<head>
<META NAME="keywords" CONTENT="keyword phrase 1 here,
keyword phrase 2 here, keyword phrase 3 here">
</head>
```

A finished META tag will look like this:

```
<head>
<title>Your Page Title Goes Here</title>
<meta name="description" CONTENT="Your web page description
goes here.">
<META NAME="keywords" CONTENT="keyword phrase 1 here,
keyword phrase 2 here, keyword phrase 3 here">
</head>
```

There may be other tags or scripts in this section with the title, description and keywords but this will give you a basic idea of what it should look like.

Note: Head tags have an opening and a closing to the tag. note the / mark on the closing head tag. This marks this tag as the closing tag or the end of the tag.

Heading Tags

Heading tags are something I use often. Typically I use the page title or (something very similar) in an H1 tag and very similar topics/keywords in H2 and H3 tags.

Heading tags are supported by major browser types/search engines. Heading tag html code is very simple, it looks like this:

```
<h1>heading 1 text goes here</h1>
<h2>heading 2 text goes here </h2>
<h3>heading 3 text goes here </h3>
<h4>heading 4 text goes here </h4>
<h5>heading 5 text goes here </h5>
<h6>heading 6 text goes here </h6>
```

The above heading tags 1-6 are also in order of importance for search engines. A heading 6 tag <H6></H6> is not as important as a heading 1 <H1></H1> tag.

Inserting text in heading tags is usually not an option in many do-it-yourself website creation programs but is available in programs like Microsoft FrontPage and Expression Web. If you are using a do-it-yourself service you will want to find out how to edit html to insert your most important keywords within the brackets of each of the heading tags. Don't put too much text in a heading tag, keep the heading tags like a page title, short and with the major keywords at the start of the heading in a short phrase or sentence.

Most times the heading tags 1-3 work just fine without using all available heading tags. Start with the page title in an H1 tag at the top of the page above the page text. Use the H2 heading tag as a paragraph title as you make you way down the page. I use the H2 tag multiple times on each page when I use it as a paragraph title and have had decent luck using this technique. However, I do not recommend using the H1 tag more than once on a web page.

Alt Tags & Link Title Tags

There are some parts of a website that will accept the use of Alt tags and Title tags. Alt tags are used for images and title tags are used for links.

Alt tags are an alternate description that can inform people of the description of an image. For example, A visually impaired reader using a screen reader program will hear the alternate text read to them by their screen reader since they are unable to see the image. Alt tags can also be a good place to stick a few keywords, but don't abuse the alt tag and remember that people who are visually impaired use this and it can confuse them if it was just stuffed with repetitive keywords.

Here is an example of the html for an image with an Alt tag:

<img alt="Photo of a blue sky on a clear day." src="http://www.YourWebsite.com/images/blue_sky_clear_day.jpg" width="200" height="100" />

The title tag for a hyperlink (not to be confused with link anchor text) from my research offers little or no benefit for the purpose of SEO, but I do use it. Might be wishful thinking but I use it for a few keywords while still keeping it simple and useful as a title tag. The title tag is meant to expand on what can be found when the user clicks the link. Many browsers will have a little pop up window appear when a visitor's mouse in hovered over the link and it will display the title the webmaster entered for that link.

Here is an example of the html code for a title tag being used in a link:
<a href="http://www.yourwebsite.com" title="Title Goes Here!">http://www.yourwebsite.com</a>

Use the title tag correctly, but stick in a few keywords. Definitely don't go crazy with it or it will look like spam and can hurt your site. Be descriptive and accurate.

Site Maps

Site maps are a way of giving search engines a virtual "map" of your website. Search engines will crawl your site map and follow the links to the pages and if the pages are accepted, they will be included in the search results.

Every time I have made a site map, I can honestly say I didn't see any major jumps on search engines. So don't expect a miracle with a site map but it is a good idea to have one.

Site maps are great for sites that don't offer a detailed navigation with lots of links. I tend to create websites with a lot of links in the navigation, this may be the reason I have not seen much extra benefit with the use of site maps.

If you have a large website, I would recommend buying a program that will generate the site map files for you automatically. It makes short work of a daunting task. A company called Coffee Cup makes an inexpensive solution for a site map generator.

Be sure you have a Google Webmaster Tools account so you can submit your site map to Google.

Linking

Linking is an important part of SEO. When done properly it can be a very useful asset to your website. The following sections are broken down by each type of linking.

Link Popularity

Link popularity is the measurement of not just how many other websites are linking to your website but the quality of those links. Some SEO's may disagree with that statement, but I truly believe quality over quantity when it comes to getting links to your website.

Increasing your link popularity is a major part of SEO. Getting links from important websites is key. Links from less popular websites are good too, but getting links from some of the big hitters on the Internet offers much more of a benefit to your website. Let's say you get 10 links from various small mom and pop gardening centers and a link from a major home improvement center's website to your leaf rake website. Your website would get a small credit and possibly a little move up on your search engine rankings for the mom and pop shop links and a decent boost on search engines for the major home improvement center's website link. Good luck getting such a link, but you get the picture.

Think of link popularity like high school. If you had one friend maybe you were a nerd, but if you had 200 friends then you were voted most popular in the yearbook. The same goes on the Internet, but online the quality of your "friends" matters more than the quantity. On second thought, looking back at high school I suppose the same applied there too. Quality links are important!

As far as what sites to get links from do yourself a favor and stay away from sites that have a ton of links on them as they may be considered "Link Farms." Link farms are known to search engines and do not do well and pass some of that junk onto your site which could actually harm your website.

Get links from quality websites that are related to your content. Don't ask a shoe store for a link to your leaf rake website. It offers no benefit to the reader and search engines know the two sites are unrelated and all efforts are lost. Spend your time wisely and get quality, related links! Where do you find such links? You will need to put some effort into this and maybe start a list of who to target for links. Consider asking suppliers, your local Chamber of Commerce (if you're a member), the town or city where your business is located (you may need to sit through a town meeting, but it's worth it), nearby businesses that compliment your business, friends websites (as long as the businesses are somewhat relative), put some thought into this right away and always keep it in mind when you meet other business owners. You really need to look as every aspect of your business to find places to get links to your website.

Link Anchor Text

Link anchor text is the visible text your website visitors see on a hyperlink which they can click on. Most common is the text "click here" but using "click here" for link anchor text is not always a good SEO technique. The link anchor text should resemble the page title of the web page you're linking to. You should use your main keywords and keyword phrases of the page you are linking to as link anchor text occasionally. Why is this important? It gives search engines information about what a visitor might find once they click on the link. Make sure the text is accurate to what is actually on the page. If your web page topic is about metal leaf rakes, the link anchor text should be something similar (i.e.: "aluminum leaf rakes," "rakes," leaf rakes," "metal leaf rakes," etc). But don't overdo the use of anchor text!

Link anchor text has been an important factor in SEO but recent updates on search engines revealed that link anchor text is best to have different variations rather than using the same exact link anchor text on every link. Search engines are using this to identify if the website owner may be using link anchor text to manipulate their ranking on search engine results. In other words if you have 110 links to your website on other websites and 100 of those use the same anchor text then search engines will know you made some sort of deal with these other websites, either a 3-way link exchange or you paid for the link. They will know you manipulated the way the link is presented in some way, undermining your linking efforts. So change it up whenever possible. With some links just use the web address, "click here," different keywords, etc. The test in the paragraph around the link is also important so don't feel your anchor text must be all keywords. It just doesn't look natural to a search engine. You also want to link to other pages of your website not just your home page.

Internal Linking

I would recommend you read the sections of this book called "Content" and "Link Anchor Text" before getting too far with internal linking. It is important to create web pages that are very specific for this to work effectively.

Internal linking is the method of linking to other parts of your own website within the content on your web pages.

Let's say you have a website that sells office chairs and you're writing content about different office chairs that are available. Each time you mention different types of office chairs, there is an opportunity to make each mention of the different office chairs into a link to the specific page for each specific type of office chair.

Example:
Our office chairs are made from a variety of different materials. We offer leather office chairs, wooden office chairs and plastic office chairs...

In the above example, you would want to create links from the following text:
leather office chairs (link to leather office chairs page)
wooden office chairs (link to wooden office chairs page)
plastic office chairs (link to plastic office chairs page)

Don't link from every mention of an office chair in your content, but include a few here and there will help search engines discover those pages and reinforce the keywords used in your link anchor text. The more they are linked to from pages on your site, the more search engines will see those pages as important to your site visitors, but again don't overuse it!

Also, including each main page in your navigation or in navigation links in the footer of every page is another great way to let search engines know the web pages are important

Over-linking may cause search engines to see this internal linking as spamming, so use the technique wisely. I link to most of my pages or at least all of my main pages in the navigation. If the navigation gets too long, I create navigation in the footer of each page and put some of the links that don't quite fit in the main navigation there. First and foremost, make it user friendly.

Using the proper link anchor text is also important. The text that surrounds the link is also important. It gives search engines yet another hint to what might be found on the page the link goes to. Don't just plaster stand alone links everywhere as that won't maximize the benefits of the linking technique. Remember, always keep your website visitors in mind. Make sure the links make sense to a visitor on your website. The text that surrounds the link should be readable for your visitors but also keyword rich for the page you are sending the visitor to while maintaining a similarity to the topic on the page where you place the link.

These internal links also offer a pathway for search engines to find new content on your website. Search engine spiders crawl through your website using these types of links as well as the navigation and site map.

Search engines also determine how important a web page is by how your site links to it. If your website only links to a webpage once in the entire site, a search engine may not see that page as an important page of your website or possibly not even find it at all. So be sure to use internal linking, but use it ethically. No need to add 60 links within the content of a webpage. I would shoot for less than 10 in the content itself, plus the links in the site navigation.

You can also use this method to provide a list of links at the bottom of the web page as "Related Links" or "Related Products" or "People Who Liked This Also Liked..." and list a few related web pages under that heading.

Reciprocal linking (Link Exchanges)

Reciprocal linking (you link to my website and I will link to yours) was a widely used tactic up until about 2008, some webmasters still use it today. Webmasters used reciprocal linking as a way of getting link popularity and was mutually beneficial to both webmasters.

Search engines recognized reciprocal links and for a while it was useful, then it was just acceptable. But then like most other forms of SEO, it was being abused. Search engines began to pull back on the credit given through the use of a reciprocal link and began giving more weight to one-way links (inbound links).

Today, I see it as a complete waste of time and do not perform any link exchanges.

One-Way Links (Inbound Links)

Getting quality inbound links to your website is currently an important part of search engine optimization. Links are considered votes by major search engines. Search out websites that may think your content is worth linking to (be sure the content you created is really worth linking to before you do this). If your website sells rakes you can imagine not many people will want to link to a page with a rake on it, so you're going to have to get creative and write articles about things that are interesting or funny. Something that people will see as different, entertaining, interesting or highly informational and want to link to. Let's say you do the leg work and find out how many people die from injuries related to rakes in the US. Write a full page article with graphs and photos about the topic, then write another article about how many people are injured by rakes every year. While these articles sound stupid, they will attract attention. Somewhere, someone will search for the answers and if they have a website, hopefully they will link to your site. This is what is considered "Natural Linking." This is how search engines *want* the Internet to work. Someone thought your article was worthy of being linked to and linked to it from their website. Giving your article about rake deaths or injuries a "vote." Search engines will then use that vote to rank your website. The more (quality) votes you have, the more that article climbs on search engines and that link power will be transferred to other parts of your site. So be sure to link to your specific rake pages from these article pages. You can also contact a few webmaster who might be interested. Ask them to link to your article.

I did a private tourism website for attractions, hotels, campgrounds, etc within the state of New Hampshire. After I had hundreds of web pages with content about almost every corner of the state I contacted each town by email or phone and kindly asked for a link on their town's website. Some said yes, some said no, some went before their Board of Selectmen, some never replied. The ones that didn't reply I contacted again. If I still didn't get a reply, I mailed them a real letter (snail mail), again kindly asking for that link. I was called tenacious, obnoxious, and by one snobby NH town a spammer and a few other choice words I won't mention.

The bottom line is you have to do some heavy work getting links! It is hard work and very boring but this is what will get your site noticed. This will strengthen everything you have done and once you start getting quality links, you can watch your site climb on the search engines little by little and your other pages will also start to climb and become entrance pages of their own.

If you want to take some of the work out of it, create good, quality unique content... I cannot stress this enough. After all my years of experience this is one of my best pieces of advice for any website owner. I have many websites and the hardest ones to get links for are the commercial websites that sell everyday services or products. Tourism or recreational websites are a bit easier.

So how else can you get links?

Forums and Blogs

Join forums and blogs related to your topic and engage in conversations. Never join a forum or blog and just start plopping links in your posts and/or your signature line as it will most likely get deleted by the website owner. Make a few posts, join in a few conversations here and there and then when you see a topic that would make sense to offer your link for good information about the topic, give it a try and see how it goes. Just place a single link. Do not use any SEO tricks like anchor text or keywords around the link. Just make it look as natural and non-biased as possible. Afterwards, make a few more posts without any links. All you want to do is get your link to stay there.

Writing Articles For Other Websites

There are plenty of websites out there that you can write articles for and place your link in the footer of the article. One site I use a lot is ezinearticles.com. It is easy to use and I have gotten traffic from the articles I published

You can also approach other webmasters and ask if you can write an article for their website in exchange for a link from the article. Some webmasters will do this while other will not. This is beneficial to the website owner because they will get free content and the person who writes the article gets a free link to their website.
Your local Chamber of Commerce...
If you are a member of your local Chamber of Commerce, ask them for a link from their website. Many Chamber of Commerce websites do have a list of members.

Getting Links by Affiliation and Location

Any organizations you are a member of or are affiliate with can also be a great resource for getting free links to your website. Check with your local Chamber of Commerce. If you are a member, try asking for a link to your website.

Another great place for a free link is your local town or city website to see if they have a list of businesses. If they do, be sure to approach them for a link. If they do not, it may be worth sending a letter and requesting time to speak at a meeting requesting the addition of a "Local Business" section on their website.

Getting links to your website should always be on your mind. You should always be looking for opportunities. Networking with local businesses can also help. Help out a few businesses along the way, make some friends... friends are good for favors like getting links. Never see all of your competitors as enemies, you may be able to help each other out. 3 or 4 competitors in an industry with hundreds or thousands of competitors can help each other out, even consider 3-way/4-way linking.

3-Way/4-Way Linking

3-way linking and 4-way linking was created when search engines began to devalue reciprocal links and is still used today as a way to fool search engines to think a link exchange is a one-way link. Because it fools or deceives search engines I would consider this type of linking search engine SPAM so if you chose to use it, do so with some caution. It is difficult for search engines to recognize this type of linking and the technique does work from what I have seen in my testing.

Here's how it works...

Much like a link exchange, you approach another webmaster that offers related content as your website. You offer them a link on another website you own (and usually don't care much about) in exchange for a link to your website from their website.

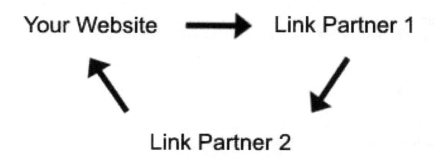

In the illustration above, you can see that the website your site links to ("Link Partner 1") is not the same site that links back to you. Link Partner 1 links to a third website that is involved in the exchange. Link Partner site 2 is where you get that valuable return link to your website.

Many webmasters that seek this type of link out will educate the recipient of their request about how this type of linking can help their website as many webmasters are not familiar with its benefits.

So if all goes well you get a link from the site you want, and to a search engine it looks like a one-way link which is worth more than a link exchange. In return you have given the other webmaster a link to their site that also appears as a one-way link to a search engine and both websites reap the benefits.

Paid Links

Paid links are something that was search engines didn't know what to do with for a while. Search engines had no way of knowing what was a paid link and what was an authentic link. In the past few years search engines have begun focusing on sites that sell links and those that buy links. Search engines watch websites like business directories that sell ad space. I believe once a directory has been identified, links leaving such a site are given little to no weight at all. I own 5 directory websites myself and they did very well until the big search engine hammer came down and I now must add nofollow attributes to these links to be an ethical directory selling ad space.

For more about paid links and the nofollow attribute, see the section called "Paid Links" in the "Black Hat SEO" chapter"

Website Stats

Website stats can be very confusing so make sure you fully understand what the terms in website stats tools (like Google analytics) really mean. The data provided in "Bounce Rate" and "Time on Site" are two topics that are often confusing to business owners.

Bounce Rates

Simply stated, a bounce rate is the measurement of people who come to your website then leave your website without viewing any other web pages on your site. They do a search or come to your site through a link, they look at the page they landed on and then either hit the back button, click on an advertisement on your site and navigate away or close the browser. I feel each of these actions all have different meanings and I feel confident assuming search engines feel the same way. It is because of this that there are many different opinions about bounce rates. Some SEO experts say bounce rates really don't really matter while others say it's an important consideration. Myself, I shoot down the middle of these opinions. I attempt to get the bounce rate percentages on the lower end (but not too low) because I feel search engines use this to measure your website. But there are different ways of looking at it. A high bounce rate might be because the user found exactly what they wanted and had no reason to keep looking through your website. Or maybe they came to your website saw a bunch of advertisements and clutter and left. Or maybe your website had the information they wanted, saw an ad for something related and wanted to buy it and left your site. All of these occurrences will show high bounce rates, but they have different meanings. So don't get too hung up on bounce rates, but if you see a high bounce rate in your website analytics, you might want to check it out to see if there is an obvious reason, maybe you will find changes that need to be made.

For website stats I use Google Analytics, so when I check bounce rates I click the bounce rate link above the stats so that it sorts the site content by the bounce rate, highest first. I look at the highest bounce rates and look at how a visitor came to that page, keywords used, time on site, etc. I also look at the content on that page myself and see if I can find a problem or diagnose the cause for the high bounce rate. Sometimes I find the high bounce rate is due to people getting a quick update on the content offered and the high bounce rate is actually a good thing. The visitor was just checking in for the latest info.

Most people agree that over 50% bounce rate is considered high and of concern, but I don't totally agree with that. Judge it with your own content. Ask yourself why would people come to this page then leave? Do you offer something that changes often and people check it often then leave? If so, your return visitors will be higher for that page and depending on how long it takes to read the changes or new images, it will also affect the time on site. If your return visitors are low and the bounce rate is high, there might be a reason for concern.

Take all things under consideration when you're looking at bounce rates, don't just judge it by the percentage. Making snap decision changes just by the percentage alone can cause you to harm your rankings. Do some investigation work before you make changes!

Time on Site

Time on site is much like bounce rates in that you have to be careful how you interpret the information. Low time on site readings might be due to people just checking-in to see the latest information. Again, use your return visitors as a guide with this. Look at the content and see if you can determine what might cause it. Is it a good thing or a bad thing? Low time on site isn't always a bad thing but it's always worth checking it and understanding the cause of it.

Black Hat SEO

The Unethical Side of Search Engine optimization

When optimizing your website, you are basically riding a thin line, closing in on spamming search engines. This is a line that you do not want to cross unless you have to and I am going to recommend not crossing it. The problem is that the line is a little gray and not so easy to detect. It is always best to use caution and don't push it. Pushing SEO too far will get your website dropped on the search results, and maybe black-listed. This is a tough thing to overcome and you might be better off starting over after such a major blow to your efforts. I have had websites banned from search engines and trust me, it no fun when you have a website bringing in money one day and the next morning you grab your coffee and sit at your desk to find it's gone from search engine results and you're broke. So take it from someone who has been there. Use your gut instinct. If it feels wrong, it probably is. Make yourself very familiar with each search engine's guidelines before you begin! Looking at it again afterwards to make sure you haven't crossed the line. I read them monthly to check for updates and remind myself where that line is.

Paid Links

Ok so you want more? Well this is where we start to really cross the line into search engine SPAM. The guru part of me is going to take over here and we're going to get a little dirty.

The details I will discuss here can get your website banned from search engines.... Make no mistake about it. So fly low and stay under the search engine radar when using this method of SEO.

Why do I bother even mentioning paid links if your website can be banned for using this method? I mention it because it's reality, some companies are doing the things I mention in this section. It's not pretty and it's not ethical but trust me it happens way more than you know. You will be seeing this more and more until search engines are able to better target those doing it and you may even find some of the large corporations making the news for "unethical SEO tactics." Keep your eye on the news, it's coming.

The only way to teach you what you need to know about unethical search engine optimization is to show you. Learning by doing is the key to understanding the information and then use it for your benefit if you desire. Whether you do it or not is your business but understanding it will help you understand what's going on around you in the SEO world and what your competition may be doing to get those top spots on the search engine results.

I have an business acquaintance that is employed as an SEO expert at a real estate company. He has a team of 10 people who work in the SEO department. All they do every day is negotiate link purchases for the company's websites. They have more than one website in expectation that they will get caught by search engines and will be banned from their search results. Having the other websites already optimized will give them something to fall back on.

How paid links started...
Once it was ok to pay for an "advertisement" on another website and have that website link to your website in your advertisement. Many advertisers knew that this advertisement also included a valuable paid link and were more interested in the link than the actual ad itself. Search engines have caught onto this practice a long time ago. Just do a search for "paid links" and you will see what I mean.

Search engines still say it's ok to buy an advertisement on another website and have a link to your website with it but they want what's called a "nofollow" tag added to a paid link's html code. A nofollow tag is a small bit of code (rel="nofollow") in the hyperlink code that tells search engines that the link is not a "vote" for the site but may be a "paid advertisement" link so no credit for the link is passed from the site your advertisement appears on to your website. It's ok for traffic to flow through that link to the advertiser's website, just not to pass any link popularity through that link.

The link with a nofollow tag looks like this:

<a href="http://www.sample.com" rel="nofollow">Visible Link</a>

Since search engines have caught onto this practice, those who are more interested in the link than the advertisement have moved on to another approach....

What many SEO companies and webmasters are doing now is buying links on other websites (usually private, non-directory websites) for their client's websites. The SEO company will usually look for websites that don't sell much ad space. Maybe they pay monthly, quarterly or yearly. They always try to negotiate a low price for the link. Common stipulations are that the nofollow attribute is *not* added to the link, therefore passing link credit to their client's website. Also that no reference is made to the link actually being an "Advertisement."

The most desirable place for these paid links are within the normal text of the home page or main page of the site on the top half or middle of the page. These links that appear within the text of a paragraph is more natural to search engines, so they are much harder to identify as a paid link and can be very beneficial to the website being linked to.

You can do this with your website too, but be very careful. As I said, you are now crossing the line and your website could be completely removed from search engines.

If you are going to spend money buying links, be sure you're doing it right! Make sure you have read the section in this book about link anchor text before starting to buy links.

This is how it works...
Search for related websites that are in a similar business that you are in but in a non-competing area. Normally small mom and pop shops are best because they could always use a few extra bucks to supplement their income.

Contact the webmaster or business owner asking if you can place a text ad on their website and you will pay them. Ask them how much it will cost. When they give you a price, try to negotiate the price down. When they won't budge anymore, tell them you will pay it but want to make sure they don't add a nofollow attribute to the link. Most small business owners won't even know what this is so usually that is not a problem. Paying monthly is best because if you pay by the year and they choose to remove your link you're pretty much screwed.

Create a small paragraph (2-4 sentences) with your link in it or maybe even 2 links in the paragraph. The paragraph of text should match or tie together the topics of both the web page where you are placing the "ad" and your web page. This will help disguise the advertisement and paid link as part of the normal website text. If you add 2 links be sure that you link to 2 separate pages of your site, maximizing your investment. Don't just place links to your home page. Make the link anchor text and surrounding text somewhat specific to the page you are linking to.

The position of the link can be somewhat important. If you can, try to get the link as high on the page ("above the fold") as possible and in the same size font. Bold is a little better as well but you don't want to make the website owner upset, so best to stay with their content and make things blend in as much as possible.

After the webmaster places the link, send the payment right away. Use a payment service like PayPal if they accept that. Don't mess around with the payment. If you show them you pay fast, they will remember it. When your renewal payment is due email them again and ask how they would like to be paid. This will give them the chance to back out before you make payment.

In all linking deals you make with other webmasters, be sure to monitor your agreement. Some webmasters will remove your link at some point, either by accident or because they don't want to link to you anymore. Rarely will the webmaster email to let you know your link was removed. So you have to be your own advocate and police your links. Create a Word doc or a spreadsheet with the location of the link, the contact person, email address and even a phone number if you can get one. Every time you pay them, be sure to note the date and method so you won't have to remember it.

Also, make sure you keep your linking strategies to yourself. If a competitor hears about what you are doing, they can (and most likely will) report you to search engines. It's easier and cheaper to sink your competitors in this game than it is to compete against them.

So what about hiring a company to purchase links on your behalf? I spent some time researching this and against my better judgment but for the purpose of this book I went along with it. Here is what I did... I took 3 spam emails I received over the course of nine months that wanted to sell me links for my website. I made purchases of $50 from all three. I got links for $10 each from two of them and $5.00 each from the other. All three told me I was getting permanent links for my one-time payment. So this sounded like a great deal. They all sent me a confirmation of where my links could be found. The sites they sent me were obviously created for the purpose of selling links. They were not very well designed at all and had a couple other links along with mine. I monitored these links for one year, checking them occasionally. At the end of the year I found that every link I had purchased was gone. They were either removed from the website, the web page was gone or the entire website was gone. Either way, I was out $150.00 and no links to show for it. The links stayed on all of the websites beyond the first 90 days which I found ironic since most credit card companies would allow you to reverse the payment if within 90 days. Possibly a coincidence. I later found that all three companies or people I purchased links from were located in India. So take from this what you will, but I would recommend you do it yourself or find a reputable local company to do it for you if you're going to do it at all.

Doorway Pages

I'm not going to get too much into this subject because it's barely worth discussing. Search engines can detect the use of doorway pages easily and this method is not used very often anymore.

In general, doorway pages are web pages that are created for something called "spamdexing" (spamming the index of a search engine).

How it works:
Doorway pages are created primarily for search engines, not humans. Normally the page heavily focuses on a single search term by using the chosen search term repeatedly in the text on the page. This is done to get search engines to rank the page higher for that particular search term. When a person uses a search engine and clicks on the link in the search results they are unknowingly taken to another page of the website that they did not intend to go to. For example, let's say the user was searching for "green dancing shoes" on a search engine. Many sites will come up that are legitimately selling green dancing shoes but if an unethical webmaster for let's say a gambling website created a page for the purpose of spamming a search engine and one of the doorway pages they created was created for the search term "green dancing shoes," their website may also appear. But when the person searching for the green dancing shoes clicks on it they are automatically redirected to a page with a promotional ad for their gambling website.

Search engines can easily detect doorway pages, which is the reason you don't see much of this anymore. Normally the page is removed from search engine's results fairly quickly.

In my opinion, it's not worth wasting your time with this technique.

Cloaking

Cloaking is very similar to doorways pages but a bit more of a fancy way of doing it. Cloaking is creating two different kinds of content, one for search engines and one for humans with the delivery of each one being determined by the visitor's IP address.

How it works:
The webmaster will create two types of content. One for search engines and one for humans, like a doorway page. But instead of forwarding the user from the keyword-rich page created for search engines and automatically sending the user to another page without their knowledge, the different content is delivered separately so that search engines never "see" the human page and humans never see the page created for search engines. The decision of which content gets delivered to search engines and the content that gets delivered to humans is determined by the visitor's IP address on the server-side. If the IP addresses matches that of a search engine bot/spider, the content will be that which was created for search engines. If the IP address is anything else, the content created for humans is delivered to the visitor.

This method is used in many different ways. Some use it to deceive search engines and deliver content that could be anything from advertising to pornography. At the very least, most times it is undesirable to the visitor.

There are some uses that are for legitimate advertising purposes, in that case it is called "IP Delivery." IP delivery is very similar to cloaking but mainly used to determine a visitor's geographic location for the purpose of delivering advertisements for local businesses in the visitor's area.

Cloaking is another method of unethical SEO that I would discourage. Most people who encounter this on your site will report you if there is a huge difference of what was shown on search results vs. what you are showing to visitors. Not to mention competitors who would gladly turn you in to get you knocked off the search results entirely.

Hidden Text

Hidden text is something that was used heavily back in the 90's. You could stuff all kinds of keywords into these hidden gems like: Towns, cities, states, etc into these (usually long) paragraphs and your website would come up for these keywords and keyword phrases nicely. At the time, search engines had no way of detecting that the text was hidden and if they did, they didn't do anything about it. Today things are much different! Making text hidden by making it the same color or even a close color (semi-hidden text) as the background where the text is located is a bad idea. If the search engines don't catch you doing it your competitor will and report you. This is a sure fire way to get bumped down on the search engine results! You may not get caught right away, but you will get caught and you will pay the consequences.

Always create unique, quality content! You will hear me say this over and over again. It is the best practice for SEO.

Other SEO Techniques

Off-site SEO is just as important as optimization of the text and code on your website itself. There are many things can be done on other websites to help your site get more traffic.

Getting links from directories and making other people aware of your website by posting it on social media sites can have a big impact on your website.

Directory Listings

There are many free directories on the Internet that you can submit your website to and get some link credit. Since the directories are free you do not have to worry about the link being a "paid link" (for more about paid links, see the section called "Paid Links"). The only directory that I would recommend being a part of is The open Directory Project at DMOZ.org. It will not make or break your site but if you're lucky enough to be included in this directory, you will get some extra traffic and will get a bump up on some search engine rankings.

One method I have used in the past to get listed on free directories was to create a very "tame" website with hardly any SEO at all and no advertisements, but offer some great detailed content. Once I felt it was perfect, I would submit it to directories and ask for links from related websites. Then, I waited a few months until everyone I wanted links from included my website on their directory and then I unleashed the SEO version of the site while maintaining the quality content on the site during the new site changeover. Why did I do this? It can help to remove the risk of being denied a listing or link on a directory or a website you wanted a link from. Once your website link is on the directory, very rarely does any webmaster or editor pull websites off and can become a permanent link that will benefit your site for many years.

Search Engine Submissions

These days there really is no need to submit your website to search engines. Search engines find your website on their own, mainly through links to your site placed on other websites, another reason why getting links to your website is so important.

See the section called "Linking" for more information.

Pay Per Click Ads

Pay-Per-Click (PPC) ads found on major search engines like Google and Yahoo are a tough business. I spent several thousand dollars on this type of advertising before I got more heavily into SEO in search of better organic search engine results.

If you decide to get into PPC advertising, be sure to watch closely, do your homework and testing. If you don't see results with the first $50-$100 you're doing something wrong. Don't keep blowing money on it until you make adjustments to correct the problems. Maybe the problem is on your website, maybe the problem is you're targeting the wrong people. You really need to work on this to get it to pay off.

Social Media SEO

Social Media is really taking off and is something you need to keep your eyes on. Sites like FaceBook have grown beyond what we all thought it would and it is starting to look like it may be taking on a more important role in SEO as time goes on.

On FaceBook, having people "like" your web pages can also help your web pages get noticed on some search engines. Bing announced in May 2011 that they are adding FaceBook "likes" to their search results. So now when you search with Bing and connect with FaceBook you will see if any of your friends "like" something that appears in your search results. You will also see how many people have "liked" the web page on FaceBook. This makes a lot of sense for Bing to make this move. Let's face it, if your friends liked the web page you most likely will too.

Bing has also added the FaceBook "like" button to their toolbar, making it a seamless experience.

Google also has their +1 button. The +1 button is similar to FaceBook's "Like" button. With this Google tool you can click the button and give the web page you're viewing a boost on Google.

I believe we will be seeing much more of this integration between social media sites and search engines in the future so be sure to add FaceBook's "like" button to all of your web pages.

Social Bookmarks

The basic idea of Social bookmarking is to have users save and manage their bookmarks and offer a collection of websites that other people might find interesting. The bookmarks are saved in a public location for everyone to view. Some social bookmarking sites are: Digg, StumbleUpon, Reddit, Del.icio.us and Slashdot just to name a few.

Social bookmarks are another way you can exploit the social networking side of the internet to help drive some traffic to your website. But be aware that bookmarking your own website for the purpose of getting more hits is considered abuse by many of the bookmarking websites.

The use of social bookmarking is fairly simple. In most cases you sign up for a free account and add some web pages you like (or even don't like). Some of the bookmarking websites also offer a comments section for the link you are adding. Getting your pages on social bookmarking sites can be a good way of getting a little free traffic. If the link you are adding is really cool, the link will get voted up and you could drive hundreds of thousands of hits to your site. But, it has to be really good stuff you are showing off to get those results!

Some will take it a step further by having many different accounts and have their friends sign up and have everyone add the same web pages. The social bookmarking websites will consider this spam and may block your accounts and/or website altogether so use this method of SEO carefully and don't overuse it. If your content is mediocre, you might still get a few hits from it.

You can also add each of the social bookmarking site's logos to your site with a link to encourage your visitors to add your website to their social bookmarks. This will work well for sites with great information and is generally considered the "correct" way to use the free service.

Remember, there is no magic bullet to SEO, its hard work. Getting visitors to your website takes a million little things that you do for your website collectively.

www.ingramcontent.com/pod-product-compliance
Lightning Source LLC
Chambersburg PA
CBHW061025050326
40689CB00012B/2707